THE

POW WOW
TRAIL

Understanding And Enjoying
The Native American
Pow Wow

Julia C. White

Illustrations
Diana E. Stanley

Book Publishing Company
P.O. Box 99
Summertown, TN 38483
800-695-2241

Cover and interior design by Warren C. Jefferson

Cover photo by Chris Roberts

ISBN 1-57067-029-3

0 9 8 7 6 5 4 3 2 1

Library of Congress Cataloging-in-Publication Data

White, Julia C. (Julia Crites), 1934—
    The pow wow trail: understanding and enjoying the Native
American pow wow / Julia C. White : illustrations, Diana E. Stanley.
        p. cm.
    ISBN 1-57067-029-3 (alk. paper)
    1. Powwows. I. Title.
E98.P86W48 1996   96-12414
394–dc20   CIP

Contents

Illustrations

INTRODUCTION

A Native American pow wow is a wonderful experience, but until now there has not been much information available to the general public on this ancient custom. That is why this book has been written—so that everyone may understand and enjoy the spectacle of the dancing and the activities going on both in the arena and on the grounds.

There are some pretty wild ideas out there on pow wows and what they are. Some answers to common questions are:

YES—pow wows are open to the public.

YES—women and children are welcome.

NO—it is not scary.

NO—there is no violence.

NO—there are no sacrifices or bloodletting.

NO—there are no drunken "Indians whooping it up."

With the growing popularity of pow wows, many communities are getting involved by hosting major events which last as long as a week. Some of these celebrations include:

Rodeos featuring Native contestants. There is a "Navajo Nation Rodeo Cowboys' Association," an "All-Indian Rodeo Cowboys' Association," and an "All-Indian Rodeo Association of Oklahoma," among others.

Mountain Man camps featuring demonstrations of blacksmithing, carpentry, tool making, gunsmithing, and other skills of the 18th and 19th centuries. The men and women who take part in these exhibits dress in authentic clothing of the era they are portraying. It's quite an educational step backward in time, especially for children.

Competitions and games which include Native-style horse racing, stickball, lacrosse, foot races, bow and arrow competitions, and other ancient fun events.

Storytellers who share timeless Native myths and legends with children (of all ages).

Demonstrations and classes on beadwork, hide tanning, cooking, finger weaving, and the making of Native crafts.

Carnival rides, clowns, and other amusements for children.

America's Ancient Race

Why is there is so much resistance among Native Americans to the word Indian? The word evolved from the term *Los Indios*, meaning "the people of the Indies," when Columbus thought he had landed there. He hadn't, and they weren't, but the word has stuck throughout the centuries for lack of a better term. "The First Peoples" or "Indigenous Peoples" is really more accurate; "Original Americans" is OK, but most Indian people prefer to be called "Native Americans," or "American Indian." It's more respectful of an ancient race which is, after all, one of the four races of man: black, white, yellow, and red.

It is important that we remember our geography and realize that the Americas stretch from the sub-Arctic to the tip of South America, and that "America" is far more than just "The United States of America." All of America is the home of the Native American, and a pow wow is one event where you may see people from North, Central, and South America gathered in one place, with a common purpose—the celebration of their heritage.

Nations and Tribes: What is the difference?

There is a difference. I'll explain by using the analogy of the government structure in a state. A Native American Nation is the sum total of a particular culture, lifestyle, and belief system of a group of people (the state). The large Nations were divided into tribes, or bands, or clans, depending upon the history and language of the people (the counties in a state). The tribes were further divided into villages (the towns), and each village had its chief (the mayor). For example, there is the Sioux Nation which is made up of many different tribes such as the Oglala, the Teton, the Brule, the Lakota, etc.

The Story Teller

Mountain Man

Potlatch Dancer

The Potlatch

Authors note: *The information presented here was gathered from comprehensive and reliable sources, and discusses the ancient celebrations called "Potlatch." Today (1996) this term has been applied to a heated political battle over control of the natural resources in some areas of the Pacific Northwest. This discussion is not about that political struggle but about the ancient Native American Potlatch celebration.*

Certainly the most unusual form of pow wow held on this continent is the Potlatch, a custom practiced on the Pacific Northwest coast from Southern Oregon to Northern Alaska. The accumulation of personal possessions and wealth was not a way of life to the Native American. Their life revolved around the good of the whole, and families took care of each other for whatever their needs were. Very often, the most revered person in the village, such as the medicine person, chief, or shaman, was the poorest in terms of personal belongings, because their needs were taken care of by the entire village.

An exception to this way of life were the Native Americans of the Pacific Northwest. Personal possessions were the most important elements in their lives. All things were guarded and treasured, from ceremonial items to everyday utensils and tools. The accumulation of "things" was the measure of personal wealth and status in the tribe or clan.

The Northwest Native Americans also collected wealth as a clan project. This gave every member of the tribe the opportunity to share in the glory and prestige of the group as a whole. The sole purpose of this massive collecting of material goods was to GIVE IT ALL AWAY.

Many clans could afford to host only one Potlatch in a lifetime. The decision on when this event would take place was made by the highest ranking member of the clan, after much discussion among the other members. Once it was determined that there were enough goods for the Potlatch, and a date was agreed upon, the efforts of the entire village turned to preparations for the gathering.

At least two other clans were invited as guests, and when they were chosen, messengers were immediately dispatched to give the news to the chiefs of those clans. Distance was no barrier, and certainly no consideration, in determining which guests were invited. Part of the duty of the host clan was to house and feed the guests for the duration of the Potlatch. Guests could number in the hundreds, and the ceremony last up to twelve days!

While the hosting clan members set about making ready for the big event, the highest ranking individual, who would act as the central figure and spokesman, began his own preparations. For a full year before the date, complex spiritual rituals took place daily to assure that he would be worthy of his responsibilities.

Of equal importance to host and guests alike was the dancing and singing which continued throughout all the festivities. Regalia was made as spectacular as possible, and the dancers themselves rehearsed endlessly to make them perfect in all respects.

The arrival of the guests signaled the beginning of the potlatch, and the eating, singing, and dancing got underway immediately. After several days of merrymaking, the tone of the potlatch took a more somber turn with the honoring of the ancestors and the dead. Following this began the final act—the giving of gifts.

Copper was the symbol of the greatest wealth of all, and the tribal chiefs of the visiting clans were presented with ornate gifts made of copper. From the chiefs down, each and every member of the guest clans received gifts of equal value befitting their standing in the clan. For example, if the wood-carvers were to receive blankets, and there were 400 wood-carvers present, then 400 blankets were given. As each gift was given, its history, value, and significance was explained in great detail. The gift was accepted with much gratitude expressed.

The intricate customs of the Potlatch varied from tribe to tribe, but they shared many common elements. In some extreme cases, after the last gift was given and the last speech made, the highest ranking member of the hosting clan, who had been the central figure and spokesman for the celebration, invited the visiting clans to DESTROY HIS HOUSE. Yes, you read it right! To refuse would have been an unthinkable insult, so . . . the house was destroyed, and the resulting shambles burned. There are photographs in research books covering this practice.

Needless to say, the reaction to this ceremony by European settlers and Christian missionaries was outrage. Convinced that they had witnessed the most wasteful, savage, and heathen behavior possible, the government of Canada took steps to outlaw the Potlatch custom. Laws were passed in 1884 which made the Potlatch illegal, and which created penalties for its observance. But the laws didn't work; the potlatch was practiced in secret. In 1895 the existing laws were amended and made even stronger, with even more severe penalties. This didn't work either and the Potlatch was only driven deeper and deeper "underground."

As historians and anthropologists began to study the lives and habits of the indigenous peoples of this area, they realized that ancient customs would not be abandoned, regardless of laws and penalties. As Canadian law was amended and rewritten over the years, the Potlatch was mentioned less and less. Regulation of the Potlatch has finally disappeared from the Canadian Code of Law altogether.

The Potlatch ceremony is still practiced in the Pacific Northwest, though not in the extreme form of the early days. Today's Potlatch is usually held as a celebration for a special event, and includes all the members of an extended family. While gifts are still given, the celebration more closely resembles a giveaway as compared to the more radical practices of old. Even in its more modern observance, the spirit of the Potlatch is alive and well. I would encourage you to read more about the roots of this tradition. The art and the crafts of this part of the country are not found anywhere else, and the traditions of these people were just as unique. It is a fascinating study for those interested in the "old ways."

I
Overview

Crow Elder

What is a Pow Wow?

If you have never been to a pow wow, you've missed an exciting, amazing, and moving experience. If you have been to a pow wow, you probably wondered what it was all about. The information presented here will help you understand the customs, the clothing, and the dances, and to enjoy your step back in history.

The word "pow wow" is a European adaptation of the Algonquin term "Pau Wau," which referred to the tribal medicine men and spiritual leaders. This term was expanded to mean the entire gathering of tribes, and was gradually accepted by the Native Nations as their understanding of English grew.

Originally these gatherings, which were held in a location central to the participating Nations, were held two times a year: in the spring after the winter thaw and in the fall after the harvest and last big hunt of the year, before the winter snows.

The spring gathering was an important event. It was a welcome chance to celebrate after the long winter months of having to stay close to home. It was also the opportunity to trade the many items that had been made over the winter months with other tribes.

The fall gathering was important because it was necessary to trade for the food staples, game, and fruit of the harvests. This gathering was a matter of life and death for those who had not had a good harvest, for it was here that the essentials to sustain the people over the coming winter were available.

The tribes traveled great distances to take part in the pow wows, for they were important gatherings for social and political reasons as well. Individual feats of bravery and outstanding achievements were honored. Betrothals were announced, weddings were performed, births were celebrated, and deaths were mourned. Meetings were held among the tribal elders, and decisions were reached which would affect the lives of the people during the coming year.

There was much feasting and dancing but, originally, only the warriors danced. Their dances told the stories of their victories, both in battle and in the hunt, and of their personal accomplishments.

Pow Wow Protocol

When you attend a pow wow, it is important to remember that you are an observer of ancient ceremonies and traditions that have survived every possible adversity. Here are things you need to know for proper behavior:

1. UNDER NO CIRCUMSTANCES ARE ALCOHOL OR DRUGS ALLOWED ON POW WOW GROUNDS. Alcohol is the greatest curse ever visited on the Native American, and it will not be tolerated. If you come to a pow wow drunk or bring alcohol or drugs, you will be escorted out by tribal security. If you can't stay sober for a few hours, then you're in the wrong place.

2. The area for dancing and ceremonies is called the arena, and its boundaries are usually marked by hay bales set in a circle. There is a sheltered area, which can either be in the form of an arbor, or simply a canopy, which designates a resting place for the elders, the dancers and singers, and the pow wow officials. Take care not to sit in these places. They are easy to identify if you pay attention.

3. It is common to see tipis and lodges set up on the grounds. THESE ARE NOT OPEN TO THE PUBLIC. Pow wow participants live in these tipis during the gathering, and they are, in fact, their homes for the duration. Please respect their privacy. Tipis and other structures set up for classes and demonstrations will be clearly marked. If a map or guide to the area is offered, it would be a good idea to get one.

4. Once the dance arena has been blessed with sage and prayer it becomes spiritual ground. Do not walk across the arena, and don't allow your children to run into the arena. You will be chastised by the announcer or other pow wow officials. I can think of no safer place for children than a pow wow, but that should not be a signal for them to run wild and be disrespectful.

5. DON'T TAKE PICTURES AT RANDOM—EITHER STILL SHOTS OR VIDEO. Some large pow wows require that you register your camera. The announcer will tell the audience when pictures are permitted, SO PAY ATTENTION. I have seen cameras confiscated and film destroyed because people did not follow the rules and take instructions seriously. If there is a particular dance you want to photograph, ASK PERMISSION OF THE ANNOUNCER. If he says no, give it up. Some dances are sacred and are never to be photographed. If you see a dancer who is especially striking, ask if you may take a picture, AFTER THEY LEAVE THE ARENA. It would be a courtesy to take their name and address and send a print of the photo. Human kindness and consideration are always long remembered and deeply appreciated.

Protocol for pictures is different depending upon the part of the country you're in and the customs of the pow wow committee. If you see videos being taken by professional-looking camera crews, chances are they represent a Native organization which sells pow wow videos, or they may be newspaper and magazine photographers who have gotten permission and clearance before the event. Be wise and be cautious—ask first.

6. A dancer's clothing is REGALIA, not a costume, and it is a prized possession. Some regalia has been handed down through the generations and is priceless. When a dancer decides to "come out" in a particular style, the regalia reflects the spirit and customs of the people being honored. This is no small decision, and a "coming out" ceremony for a new dancer is a cause for great celebration. The regalia is handmade, usually by the dancer, friends, and family. Every article has special meaning, and it takes years to collect items until the regalia is complete. DO NOT EVER TOUCH A DANCER'S REGALIA without permission. The regalia is an expression of spirit and has been prayed over and blessed. Honor it, the person wearing it, and the living history it represents.

7. Finally, put aside the Hollywood image of what an "Indian" looks like. Native Americans come in all sizes, shapes, and colors. From a milky skinned, blue-eyed blond or a green-

21

eyed redhead, to the dark brown and the black, they are all Native Americans in their heritage, blood, and heart. Some are tall and stately, some are short and stocky; some have long, angular faces, some have round faces; some have round eyes, some have almond shaped eyes, and some have a definite Oriental slant to their eyes. As you learn about Native history and anthropology, you will become aware that these physical characteristics are a clear indication of the lineage of that person's heritage. Do not be so insensitive as to ask someone if they are "Indian," or "how much Indian are you, anyway?" Would you ask a native of Japan "how much Japanese are you, anyway?" Don't scoff, it's happened to me—look, learn, and enjoy.

Be Comfortable

A pow wow is no place to dress to impress. You will impress no one, and you will be miserable and grouchy and sorry you came.

The best time to go to a pow wow is around 3 p.m. on Saturday, and you should plan to stay late. By then the competition should be in full swing, and you will see the most outstanding dancers. There is a supper break around 6 p.m. which would be a good time to shop at the vendor booths circling the arena. You will also get to see the second Grand Entry which usually begins around 7 p.m. and which signals the beginning of the night session.

Most pow wows are held in the country away from the conveniences we all take for granted. Some pow wows are held in doors, in parts of the country where weather could be a problem. It is also getting popular to have pow wows on church grounds, at college campuses, and various other locations in cities where there is enough room.

The following tips will help you to get the most pleasure from your pow wow experience.

1. If you're in a hurry, don't go. When you enter the grounds, sometimes called "stomp" grounds, you're on "Indian time." Forget clocks and schedules—be in the moment, in every sense of

the word.

2. Take water, water, and more water; some to drink yourself, some to share with someone, and some to keep yourself cool. Take a washcloth in a container with a small amount of water so you can wipe your hands and face. Be aware of your body temperature, and don't get overheated. I have seen people pass out from heat exhaustion because they were not properly prepared.

3. Wear loose, comfortable clothing that does not bind. Be conservative, a pow wow is not the place to wear a mini-skirt, short shorts, or a scanty Bikini top.

4. Remember that you're going to be walking on dusty, uneven ground and weaving your way through crowds of people. Wear comfortable walking shoes or sneakers that give your feet plenty of support and protect your toes if stepped on.

5. Be sure your children are dressed the same way. Cute sun suits lead to terrible sunburns, and sandals invite bruised toes, twisted ankles, and rock bruises. Take a hat to protect your child's head and face from the sun. If your child is a toddler, or younger, take the stroller. Be sure children know where the announcer's booth is. If you should get separated, tell them to go to the announcer and ask him to call you over the loudspeaker system. Don't panic if you lose someone. They're most likely safe—you just can't see them.

6. Take aluminum folding chairs to sit on, and if you have an umbrella you can attach to the chair, take it. There is little to no natural shade, and you will welcome that umbrella. Stake out your spot somewhere around the arena, outside the hay bales or arena markers, and plant your chair. Be aware of the reserved areas we talked about earlier. Don't be rude and sit in someone else's chair or in a spot that is marked with someone else's belongings.

7. Take a hat for yourself and enough sunscreen for everyone. There will likely be no shelter, and the sun can be merciless. The temperatures can get extreme. Now don't wimp out; look at what the dancers are wearing and the heat they're danc-

ing in. They don't have summer light regalia!

8. Take toilet paper. Yes, I'm serious. There are portable toilets on the grounds, but if there is a large crowd, the toilet paper won't last long. Find the portables early so that when the need arises you'll know where they are. If the crowd is large you know there will be lines for the toilets. Be sure you give yourself enough time to make it.

9. Take sweaters for everyone. Once the sun goes down it gets cool, and after the heat of the day it's easy to catch a chill. Be prepared for nightfall with a good flashlight. It gets very dark on the pow wow grounds. Most of the time the only light comes from portable lighting in the immediate vicinity of the arena and the vendor booths. A good flashlight will keep you from stepping in holes, tripping, or otherwise stumbling around.

10. There are food vendors that sell a variety of food which is cooked fresh on the spot. This is the place to try an Indian Taco, or Indian Fry Bread, or any of the other Native foods offered. If you're on a special diet, or eat only certain kinds of food, take it with you. A cooler with your own food and drinks will ease your mind.

11. If you take your pet, keep it on a leash. Many vendors and participants travel with large dogs, many wolf hybrids, for their personal safety, and to protect their many valuables. Also, if you take your pet, be considerate of others, and take your pooper scooper and clean up any mess it makes.

12. Some pow wows have camp grounds and space for RV's with trailer hook-ups, and cooking pits. The promotional flyers usually mention whether or not camping is permitted. If they don't, call and ask. It is common for tents to be pitched around the grounds, but the earth may not be solid enough for a motor home. Don't assume—ASK before you go.

13. If you plan to stay in a motel, be wise and call ahead. The nearest town may be miles away, and the accommodations may be very limited. Rooms could be scarce because of people coming into the area for the event, both participants and visitors. If you are not familiar with the surroundings call the near-

est Chamber of Commerce, or get yourself a motel directory, and find out for sure what's available. MAKE RESERVATIONS.

Native American Gatherings

There are different types of gatherings that call themselves pow wows; some are and some are not. There are large events which are really arts and crafts shows with Native exhibition dancers. The arts and crafts are beautiful, and while there are usually not as many dancers, it is a pleasant experience. If this is all you can get to or all that is available in your area, go; you will get the flavor of a Native American gathering.

There are small, local, one-day events which are more traditional social gatherings. It is a real pow wow, with dancing, food, and items for sale, but without competition dancing, elaborate settings, or formal structure.

The pow wows discussed here are on the grand scale: three-day and longer events, which draw thousands of spectators and have many tribes represented. There could be hundreds of dancers and many drums from all over the United States, Canada, and Mexico. The participants compete for prize money, which can often be thousands of dollars.

This is the inter-tribal competition pow wow which is a glorious and exciting event to watch and be part of. This type of pow wow began in the early 1900s. Until that time, dances were performed only by elite warrior societies for the benefit of tribal elders and tribal dignitaries.

The dancing often goes into the early hours of the morning. Dancers are judged on the authenticity of their regalia and dance movements; the position and movement of their heads, bodies, and feet; how they use the ceremonial tools carried in their hands; and how their dancing begins, flows, and ends with the beat of the drum. There are many dancers who make their living traveling the pow wow trail and entering competitions, so you can be sure that you're going to see the best of the best.

Pow Wow Officials

The Announcer's role is like a master of ceremonies, and he explains the activity taking place in the arena. The announcer is responsible for keeping events moving in an orderly and timely manner, and he calls the dancers to prepare for dancing. He also notifies the drums of the order and type of song they will play. He makes announcements of general interest to those present and even tells jokes when there is time. Any questions you have should be directed to him.

The Arena Director oversees the activities inside the dance arena and works closely with the announcer in making sure events move in a smooth and orderly way. He also guards and protects any eagle feather which may drop until it can be retrieved in the traditional manner of the hosting tribe. The dropping of an eagle feather has different meanings from tribe to tribe and Nation to Nation. When a feather falls, all dancing stops until it is retrieved by the person chosen for this ceremony. In some cases, the fallen feather is taken to the grave of a veteran or a respected elder; in other cases, it is simply returned to the dancer who was wearing it.

The Whip Man assists the arena director with care of the area just outside the dancing arena. His primary function is to see to the care of the elders, making sure they have comfortable seating, shade, water, food, and whatever else may be needed. The Whip Man usually carries a small whip of braided leather, and when it is pointed at you, you must dance! In times gone by, if you did not honor his command, you had to pay him money. While this is not usually the case today, it can happen, especially if yours is a familiar face. It's all in good humor.

Pow Wow Singers/The Drum

The drum and its singers are the heartbeat of all the Nations and certainly of a pow wow. It's a little confusing, but the drumming teams, which can make or break a pow wow, are called "singers." All members of the drumming team make up "the drum." The skill of the dancer goes out the window if the drum does not hold its rhythm, or falters, or is out of beat, or the sing-ers are not in sync with the drum. I have seen dancers in the arena gradually stop their movements because they could not follow the drum. An expert drumming team is a joy to dancers and audience alike. They are in great demand, travel far and wide, and are paid well for their expertise.

When there is an outstanding drum, it is not unusual to see the dancers gradually gather around the drum, still dancing, until all dancers have congregated. This is the way to pay honor to the pow wow drum. It's very moving.

The dancers may blow eagle bone whistles, which tells the drum to continue for another round. Eagle bone whistles are only given to those who have distinguished themselves at the Sun Dance, or in service to their people, or in some way that has brought the person to the attention of tribal elders. To be awarded an eagle bone whistle is an honor, and to have it blown for a drum gets considerable attention.

Each dance has its own drumming speed and rhythms. One rhythm you will NEVER hear is the ONE, two, three, four; ONE, two three, four; that is sometimes heard in movies about the old West. This rhythm was invented by the motion picture industry for John Wayne westerns. It is not an authentic beat.

A lot of the druming and chanting you will hear at a pow wow are traditional songs that have been handed down over the generations. They are usually sung in the language of their ori-gins. This can be unnerving to the unsuspecting ear. I witnessed an example of this during the filming of the Steven Seagal film "On Deadly Ground."

More than 300 Native Americans were hired, representing over 200 tribes from Alaska, Canada, and the United States. Each of us wore our personal tribal clothing, and we represented a true gathering of Nations. While most of the wonderful scenes showing this assemblage ended up on the cutting room floor, we were all present for the three days it took to shoot this particular scene. There was a drumming team among us, and we gathered around the drum in an indoor garden during breaks in the film-ing. Of course, when a drum is around, it is played, and when you have a drum playing around Native Americans, you have dancing. We had a blast!

The next day I noticed an unusual quiet among the non-Native crew members and cast. I asked one assistant director if he enjoyed the drumming and dancing. He answered that all of the Native Americans gathered in one place, with all their different regalia, and the gentle rustle of the rattles, bells, and feathers, was having a definite effect on the crew. He said that he was not able to sleep the night before because he could not get the singing out of his head. It had sounded like crying to him. They were all relieved to see us go when our assignment was finished.

New songs are written constantly which reflect world events and which poke fun at society. Listen carefully during social dances, inter-tribals, and drumming exhibitions. These songs are usually sung in English, and if you pay attention, you will understand the words. I really cracked up at one large pow wow when I realized the very solemn drum rhythm being played had words which said, "Micky Mouse, and Minnie Mouse, and Goofy too. They all live in Disneyland and work there too."

Drum and Singers

Made of various skins, but usually deer, the drum is a living thing which is honored and cared for with respect. Many Native Nations refer to the drum as the "horse," because it carries their spirit into other realms and other times. "Ride The Horse" is an expression which means to free your mind and allow your body to feel the power and pulsations of the drum, so that your spirit can travel. You can do this—try it—it's amazing.

The pow wow drum is often called the "Mother Drum." These drums are usually quite large, with enough room for 12 or more singers to sit comfortably around them. The drum is suspended from a wooden frame in order to keep it slightly off the ground. This allows the music and vibrations to flow into Mother Earth and to be returned from Mother Earth, to resonate through your feet and into your heart.

There are at least two host drums: a Northern, a Southern, and sometimes a Canadian. They are responsible for keeping the competition flowing in an uninterrupted manner, with no gaps in the music. "Northern" and "Southern" do not refer to the part of the country the drum comes from but rather to the type of music and songs they play. The former is high-pitched and played fast; the latter is low in pitch and played slow. There is no competition between the host drums.

Drum teams will travel many miles to take part in the festivities, and all are welcome to join in. Visiting drums are given a place to play in the rotation of songs and dances. Sometimes there will be competition between visiting drums, and the atmosphere can become quite "charged" when this happens.

Gourd Dance

The Gourd Dance is not a competition dance. It is performed by veterans who have served in the many armed conflicts of the United States. The men wear the regalia of their tribe but with added memorabilia of their battle campaigns, such as bandoliers made of shell casings. They wear a blanket made of two pieces of fabric, one red and one blue, sewn together in the middle. On the blanket are sewn conduct and special award ribbons, medals, battle patches, and insignia indicating their branches of service and the roles they filled. They carry rattles in their hands which keep the rhythm of the drum.

In some parts of the country, veterans will wear their actual battle fatigues, camouflage, or other uniforms. It is all a respectful way of honoring their contribution to the safety of this country. Women members of the auxiliary dance in an outer circle behind the men and dance in honor of their relatives, both living and dead, who served in our wars.

The Gourd Dance is a solemn, prayerful dance and is not customarily photographed. It honors the bravery, valor, and self-sacrifice of the survivors, and it honors the memories of those who have passed on.

Grand Entry

The Grand Entry marks the official beginning of the pow wow. The Grand Entry procession enters the arena from the east, as all dancers do. On the Medicine Wheel, east is the direction of new beginnings, birth, rebirth, and awakenings. Everyone will be asked to stand during the Grand Entry. Men are asked to remove any head gear, unless it carries an eagle feather.

Leading the Grand Entry is the Eagle Staff, which represents the spiritual symbol of all Native Nations, followed by the American flag, the Canadian flag, the POW-MIA flag, and the Tribal flag of the pow wow host. Being a flag bearer is a great honor that is not taken lightly by the pow wow committee or the persons selected.

Next in the procession are the Head Dancers in each division and title holders from other pageants and events. The head dancers are chosen by the pow wow committee because of their expertise and standing in the dance competition. They are held as an example for other dancers and take part in the judging. They are followed by notable elders and invited dignitaries.

Next in line are the men competition dancers: traditional, grass, and fancy. Then come the women competitors: traditional, fancy shawl, and jingle dress. Next up are the junior boys and girls, in the same order as the adult men and women, and the tiny tot girls and tiny tot boys, again in the same order as the adult men and women. Following the competition dancers are the specialty and exhibition dancers who perform for the pleasure of those present—they do not compete for prize money.

The procession winds around the arena in the direction of the sun (clockwise) with the dancers showing off their regalia and footwork to the spectators, indicating that they are ready to begin. After all dancers have entered the arena and made a complete circle there is a Flag Song, followed by an invocation blessing the gathering. Many times, the invocation is spoken in the Native tongue of the pow wow host tribe or an invited elder. Even though you won't understand the words, please give this prayer the same respect you would any prayer. Keep the children still and refrain from talking, whispering, or getting restless.

Following the invocation, the Eagle Staff and all flags are positioned either in the center of the arena or at the announcer's booth. The Eagle Staff is always higher than all flags, signifying the First Nation. Once the Staff and flags are set to rest, the pow wow is ready to begin . . . and YOU CAN NOW SIT DOWN!

The Grand Entry

Gourd Dance

Headaddresses

II
Competition Dances

Blackfoot Man

COMPETITION DANCES

Fancy Dance

The men's Fancy Dance evolved when pow wows began to be open to the public and competition dancing began. This dance is often referred to as a "war dance," but I have found nothing in history to support this description. The Fancy Dance is said to have originated in Oklahoma, where Native dancers were asked to make their regalia more colorful and exciting for the white spectators. Thus, the brilliant feathers of many colors, bearing long streamers which fly in the wind, were introduced. To give the regalia more flash and sparkle, sequins, mirrors, and other decorations are being added, particulary by the dancers who perform at night, under spotlights.

The Fancy Dancer is easily identified by his brilliant regalia and the double bustle of feathers. One bustle is hung from straps at the waist. The other is mounted on blocks of wood or other sturdy bracing and suspended between the shoulder blades. Their regalia also includes anklets of angora fur with sheep bells attached, a ribbon shirt, a beaded yoke, a belt, and silver or copper arm bands and cuffs. On their heads they usually wear a headband and a roach of porcupine quills that carries a spinner with one or two feathers resting inside. Can you imagine the weight of all this?

The Fancy Dance is an original, free-form dance which shows off the athletic ability, acrobatics, and endurance of the dancer. It features leaps, spins, and fast footwork, all in time to the drum. In dance-offs, to test and challenge the dancer, the drum will often get faster and faster, stopping and starting without warning. The dancer must keep up with the drum's rhythms, stops, and starts or lose points in the competition.

Fancy Shawl Dance

This is a women's dance which began in the early 1930s, making it a new tradition in competition dancing. There are two stories about its origins.

One is that a butterfly lost her mate in battle. Grief stricken, she withdrew into her cocoon (her shawl). She vowed to travel the world stepping on each stone she came across until she found beauty in one and could start her life over.

The other story tells that women gradually gave up the buffalo robes and heavy blankets they wore as the lighter weight shawls came into their hands from European traders. The dance was developed as a way to show off their beautiful, new clothing.

Whichever story you like, the movement of the shawl in the dance does resemble the motions of a butterfly's wings. The dresses are traditionally made of satin or taffeta and are knee length. On the feet they wear heavily beaded moccasins and matching leggings. Elaborate beadwork is also worn in the hair and on yokes placed over the lightweight dresses. The colors of the dresses and beadwork usually reflect the colors and designs of the woman's tribe. Most important is the elegant shawl with its long, flowing fringe which is opened and closed often during the course of the dance.

The steps of the dance are all original, fast, and athletic, with the focus on spins and twirls with the shawls. An expert Fancy Shawl Dancer appears to never touch the ground, as her footwork is so light and fast, and the motion of her body so fluid. Again, her feet must move in rhythm with the tempo of the drum, stopping and starting when it does. She must end her dance on the last beat with both feet on the ground and her arms at her side.

Grass Dance

The Grass Dance is ancient and has many names and stories about its origins and purpose from Nation to Nation. One version says that the Grass Dance was the first dance when pow wows were conducted in the ancient manner. The dancers were the great warriors of the tribe who wore the scalps of their enemies hung around their waists as they danced the stories of their battles. If there was an ancient war dance, this would seem to be a more accurate description of the original Grass Dance. Over the years the scalps gave way to grass and then yarn, and the Grass Dance became the first social pow wow dance when the gatherings were opened to public view.

Another version tells that the grass dancers were tribal members called in to tamp down the tall grass before a village or camp site was set up and that they wore streamers of grass hung from their waist. The dance itself, and especially the footwork, does create the impression of weaving through tall grass and smoothing it down.

The Grass Dance is the most beautiful and graceful of all the men's dances. It emphasizes long, fluid body motions which extend into the legs and feet to emulate waving prairie grass. The mark of an expert Grass Dancer is his ability to keep his head nodding from side to side or up and down, in time to the drum beat, in order to keep the feathers on his roach headdress constantly spinning. It is an original, free-form dance.

The Grass Dancer's regalia is made up of an ornate yoke which slips over the head and rests on the shoulders from which hangs the flowing yarn. The dancer wears a belt, beaded moccasins, beaded wrist cuffs, and a bandana around his head topped with a porcupine roach. Upon the roach rests a spinner with two feathers. (It is said that the two feathers in the spinner represent two braves returning to the village telling stories of their adventures.) From the shoulders, chest, wrist, and waist hang very long strands of yarn in the colors of the dancer's tribe or colors of his choice. The yarn represents the grasslands and is so thickly attached that the dancer's entire body seems to be covered. A truly expert Grass Dancer seems to float on waves of yarn without a joint in his body.

Jingle Dress Dance

The design of the jingle dress follows instructions given to an Ojibwa holy man in a dream. According to legend, he was shown how to make the dresses, given the songs for the dance, and was shown how the dance was performed by four young women dancers of his village. When he woke, he told his wife of the dream. Together, they made the four dresses. He then called the four women who had danced in his dream to explain the dress and the dance to them. He presented his vision to the tribe at its next gathering.

The regalia and the dance quickly spread across the Ojibwa Nation, which extended throughout Minnesota, Wisconsin, and Michigan. In the 1920s, the Ojibwa people shared the jingle dress and its history with the Sioux Nation, and its popularity spread throughout the Dakotas and Montana. It is now preformed by women of all Native Nations throughout Canada and the United States.

The dress itself is knee length, made of fabric, and is covered from shoulder to hem with hundreds of *jingles,* "cones made from the metal lids of snuff cans." These cones are attached either to the dress itself or to rows of ribbons arranged in intricate patterns. To complete the Jingle Dress regalia, the dancers wear beaded or silver concho belts, beaded moccasins and matching leggings, a scarf at the neck, a bag or pouch over the arm, and a fan made of feathers. A feather in the hair, held in place by a heavily beaded decoration, completes the regalia.

The dance itself is fast and follows the traditional footwork originally given in the holy man's dream. There is some similarity between the dance steps and an Irish Jig in its complexity and execution. Not only must the Jingle Dress Dancer keep the rhythm of the drum, she must also keep the rhythm of the jingles, stopping on the last drum beat with both feet on the ground.

Men's Traditional Dances

These dances are as ancient as the Native Peoples themselves. The dancers represent warriors as they prepare for the hunt and for battle and as they return to dance the stories of their adventures. The face paint and body paint represent the highly personal statement of the dancer. The head gear ranges from animal pelts to a full cap of magpie feathers, depending upon the tradition of the tribe being honored by the dancer. The footwork also reflects the ancient traditions of each tribe.

Even though this is a highly traditional and regional dance, there are still guidelines for judging purposes. The body movements must be authentic for the tribe and region; the basic regalia must be authentic, and the dance steps must be executed with the rhythm of the drum.

The traditional dance is divided into two categories: Northern Traditional and Southern Straight. This is no indicator of the part of the country the dancer's tribe comes from, but a style of dancing and regalia which speaks to him and touches his heart. I know an Apache who dances Northern and a Sauk-Fox who dances Southern; this is not unusual.

Northern Traditional

Northern Traditional regalia has as its basic components a breech cloth, a breastplate made of bone, a choker made of bone, anklets made of angora fur with sheep bells above them, a belt, wide wrist cuffs, arm bands of copper or silver, moccasins, and appropriate decorations either on the head or in the hair. In the hands are carried a war shield, dance staff, a feather fan, a war weapon, and many times, a dream catcher or medicine wheel. Depending upon the tribe, regalia may also include leggings, a long-sleeved ribbon shirt, and a single bustle of feathers suspended from the waist. This dance is more physically active than the Southern Straight, but not as fast or acrobatic as the Fancy Dance.

Southern Straight

Southern Straight regalia is similar in many ways to Northern Traditional. The basic components are a breech cloth with leggings, a long-sleeved ribbon shirt with bone breastplate, a bone choker, a bandolier, a belt, arm bands of copper or silver, woven yarn garters at the knees (sometimes with bells), and usually a porcupine roach headdress supporting a single feather. In the hands are carried a medicine wheel or dream catcher, feather fan, war weapon, and staff.

The most distinctive and easily identified item of the Southern Straight regalia is a very long trailer which goes down the dancer's back to the ground. Usually made of otter fur and called a "drag," this article of clothing is decorated with beadwork and other items which have special significance to the dancer. This dance is very tightly controlled and elegant, with slow moving footwork and regal body positions.

Women's Traditional Dances

As with the men, the Women's Traditional Dance is as old as the history of Native dancing. In ancient days, women danced in a circle at the outer edge of the dance arena, so they could keep watch over the safety of the village while the men were dancing.

There are two types of regalia, Buckskin and Cloth, and two types of dance steps, Northern and Southern. The Northern style of dance is performed in one spot with the woman's body doing all the work. Her feet shift in place without actually moving very much. With the Southern style the dancer moves around the arena in a clockwise motion, in a slow, tightly controlled, and majestic manner.

Buckskin Regalia

The Buckskin regalia dress is heavily beaded in elaborate patterns on the yoke and can be knee length or ankle length. It can be two piece and has yards of flowing fringe from the arms and hem. This fringe is said to represent the continuous flow of a waterfall with its life-giving water and energy, symbolizing the perseverance of the Native mother. The fringe is kept in constant motion by the movements of the body.

The dancer's hair is heavily decorated and usually has hair wraps of fur or beaded hair ties. All manner of fine jewelry is worn in the ears, and around the neck, and on the fingers. The dancer wears beaded moccasins with matching leggings, a beaded bag or pouch over the arm, a beaded or silver belt which sometimes carries a sheathed knife, a heavily fringed shawl folded over one arm, and a feather fan.

Traditional Cloth Regalia

The Cloth Regalia dresses are usually made of trade cloth and are decorated with elk teeth, coins, cowrie shells, and dentalium shells. Many times they are also decorated with ribbon work, fine beading, or floral designs in intricate beadwork again depending on the woman's tribal customs and the part of the country she comes from. The elaborate floral work, executed in beading and/or porcupine quills, comes from the region around the Great Lakes and the states bordering Canada.

The bead work is a reflection of contact with French traders who introduced the embroidered floral designs to various Native tribes. Since they could not embroider, Native women made similar designs in beads and quillwork. The remaining accessories of the Traditional Cloth regalia remains much the same as the Buckskin regalia.

The regalia of the women dancers is breathtakingly beautiful. The intricate detail is the result of endless hours of painstaking hand work which has been taught through the generations. It's OK to stare.

Children Dancers

From the time a child is born into a pow wow family, it is carried into the dance arena by its parents. Once that child can walk and keep good balance, their dance training begins. The child dancer is dressed in miniature replicas of adult regalia, with just as much attention to detail. The dance categories they compete in are the same as the adult divisions. Yes, the children are also awarded cash prizes and other rewards, and they are very serious, indeed, about their competitions. While the children dancers are "cute," their participation is also visible evidence that this element of their heritage is being passed from parent to child; the tradition of the dance is being kept alive. It is heartwarming to see these youngsters so intent with their moves.

Competition dancing for boys and girls begins with the Tiny Tots at age 5 and under. The next division is the 6-to 11-year-old age group. Junior dancers range from 12 to 17 years old, adults from 18 to 49 years old, and Golden Age is 50 years old and over. Dancing is the Native Person's expression of thought and soul and spirit. It never stops.

Men's Fancy Dance

45

Fancy Shawl Dance

Grass Dance

Jingle Dress Dance

Northern Traditional Dance

Southern Straight Dance

Buckskin Regalia

Traditional Cloth Regalia

Tiny Tots

Tiny Tots Fancy Dance

III
Speciality and Exibition Dances

Sioux Man

SPECIALTY AND EXHIBITION DANCES

In order to give the competing dancers a rest and to break the intensity of the competition, Specialty and Exhibition Dances are sprinkled throughout the schedule. These dances bring the beauty and tradition of ceremonies from the different Native American tribes across the country to people who would otherwise never have the opportunity to enjoy them. Depending upon the part of the country you're in, you could see the following dances.

Aztec and Mayan Dancers

There are a number of troupes of Aztec and Mayan Dancers who travel the pow wow trail bringing awareness of their cultures to the general public. The regalia is ornate and magnificent, and the headdresses are towering mountains of elaborate tropical bird feathers. Their dance rhythms are set by the throbbing beat of the jungle drum. Their footwork and dance patterns are very similar to a Broadway chorus line, synchronized dancing, and line dancing. Watch for an opportunity to see them.

Corn Dance

Corn was the major staple in the diets of the Native Nations from coast to coast. East of the Mississippi River, the Corn Dance was customarily performed after the growing season to give thanks for the harvest. In the western and more arid parts of the country, it was performed to seek rain and gentle weather so the crops could flourish.

Hoop Dance

There are a number of Hoop Dancers who travel the pow wow trail. This is one of the most difficult dances of all to master. The Hoop Dancer uses from 12 to 20 hoops, which he passes over and around his body while in motion, to form intricate geometric designs and patterns. It takes years of practice and patience to become skilled in this dance.

Eagle Dance

The most honored and revered animal to all Native Nations, even above the mighty buffalo, is the eagle. The regalia of the Eagle Dancer varies somewhat in different parts of the country, but the soaring spirit of the eagle in flight is the common theme expressed by dancers from all tribes.

Animal Dances

Dances are performed to honor various animals which have great meaning to the survival of the Nations. Native Americans believe that each animal has lessons to teach humans to help them live in balance with themselves, each other, and the earth itself. Animal Dancers take on the spirit of various animals, and its body movements, to create the illusion that the animal itself is dancing. The more common animal dances are the Bear, Deer, and Buffalo. Animal Dances are widely performed across the country.

Sneak-up Dance

This is a dance of the Great Plains, usually performed by the men Northern Traditional Dancers. It tells the story of warriors cautiously moving from rock to bush to retrieve the wounded and dead who have fallen in battle. I do not know of any pow wow that allows this dance to be photographed.

Mountain Spirit Dance

Also called the Gan or Gaan Dancers, they represent the protector spirits of the Mescalero Apache. Each dancer signifies a specific spirit, with a specific mission. The bodies of the dancers are painted, and the heads and faces are covered by a hood, with eye holes cut out. On top of the hood is worn an elaborate headpiece made of wooden slats with ornate decorations and symbols painted in bright colors. In the hands are carried crosses and/or swords also made of wooden slats. In recent years, the Mountain Spirit Dancers have begun to travel the pow wow trail more often, so you might be able to catch them, especially in the Southwest.

Team Dancing

Team dancing is a new and innovative addition to the pow wow. The most outstanding I have seen was the Fancy Shawl Dance performed by two sisters, who are Canadian Cree. The sisters themselves were quite startling in their appearance, for they had skin that was the color of fine porcelain. One had blond hair with green eyes; the other had red hair with blue eyes. Their regalia had been designed for optimum effect; the blond dancer was wearing shades of pink, and the redhead dancer was wearing shades of blue. Everything was covered with intricate designs in sequins, tiny mirrors, and flashing bugle beads. I have never forgotten the spectacle of those two beautiful, young women dancing in perfect unison.

Team Dancing is a very exciting experience, and I hope it becomes more widely danced. It is strictly an exhibition dance now, but perhaps someday it will become a competition dance. It certainly should.

Blanket Dance

Exhibition dancers and visiting drums are not paid for their contributions to the pow wow, nor are they eligible for competition prize money. In order to help offset their expenses, it is common for pow wow officials, and perhaps some elders, to slowly circle the arena carrying an open blanket.

The purpose of this dance is to seek donations for expenses from all those present. All donations are welcome, from folding green, to pocket change. You are encouraged to step forward into the arena and make some contribution, however small.

Sometimes a blanket dance will be held for a person, or family, who has fallen upon financial hardship. The announcer will explain the purpose of the blanket dance. Any contribution is greatly appreciated.

Aztec and Mayan Dancers

Corn Dance

Hoop Dancer

Eagle Dancer

Bear Dancer

Deer Dancer

Buffalo Dancer

Sneak-Up Dance

Mountain Spirit Dancer

Chumash Dancer

Two Step Dance

The Chumash

Although the Chumash are not exhibition dancers, or specialty dancers, I draw special attention to them here because they are so unique in their music, dance, regalia, and heritage, and because it is a disappearing Nation. According to a Chumash elder, the last full blooded Chumash died in the 1940s. There are only nine traditional families left who are still living on the Chumash reservation in the Santa Inez Mountains of California. The story of their Nation is another of the great tragedies which came out of the settling and "civilizing" of California.

The more traditional Chumash are very withdrawn and will never get too physically close to a non-Native. They will not shake your hand, and under no circumstances will they allow themselves to be photographed. Do not be offended by their standoffish behavior; when you learn their history you will understand.

The Chumash was the largest of the California Nations and were considered the intelligentsia in that part of the country. This is not the place to go into their history, but I would encourage you to read about them at your library, or read the thumbnail account I have written in Issue 31 of *Connecting Link* Magazine.

Their music, dancing, and regalia are the same now as it was hundreds of years ago. One elder told me that this is because they were "untouched by Buffalo Bill." This means they had escaped the pressure from Europeans to change their ways to please the eyes of foreign spectators.

The Chumash stay close to their homeland, and even though some of the younger dancers are participating in more pow wows, they can only be seen in California. It is not difficult to identify them; the women wear two piece hide dresses with shallow fringe, if any, which are decorated with shells and ornaments made from shells, and the bones of sea animals. The men wear capes, wraps of feathers, and the fur of seals and otters.

The men's regalia consists of skirts made of feather down

wrapped around milkweed, weighted down at the hem with flicker feathers or finely shredded grasses. The face and body are painted red, black, and white, in abstract splashes of color, which do not seem to have any particular design. The dance steps are small and quick, as if the dancer is stepping on hot coals, and they follow a one-one-one-one rhythm that does not vary. The animals they honor with their dance are sea animals, and their body motions are fluid, undulating, and sensual, as if moving through water. Watching the Chumash dance is spellbinding, and an experience I hope you have.

I have recently learned that plans are underway to construct a living museum that will show Chumash tribal members going about their normal daily activities as they did at the turn of the century. Among other things, they plan to have the traditional Round House, brush huts, an underground ceremonial chamber, sweat houses, and many other structures that will reflect the ancient life. This undertaking is called The Red Roadrunner Village. For additional information on its progress and development contact Un-At-Kah Tasen, Inc., Post Office Box 1836, Ojai, California 93024; phone (805) 525-7824.

FUN DANCES

Don't think of Native Americans as always somber, stoic, or dead-pan. They are humorous and fun-loving, and this is reflected in their dancing. What I call "fun dances" provide comic relief from the serious competitions.

Hat Dance

The goal here is for a man to put a hat or cap on the woman of his choice—but he has to catch her first! There are no innocent bystanders here, EVERYONE is fair game. Even though I know this, and even though I watch carefully to not get caught, my guard slipped one time. I had my back turned, talking to someone, and was simply not paying attention. A dancer that I knew by sight, and who was a regular on the pow wow trail, walked around and said, "Julia, would you hold this for a minute?" and handed me a baseball cap. Without a thought, I took it. There was instant applause and laughter; someone had finally gotten me. Of course, no one laughed harder than my husband!

Once the hats are in place, the women who have been caught gather in the arena. They must execute the men's dance the announcer calls, for as many rounds as he says. You can be sure that he calls the most difficult dances, and for long enough to make the knees weak.

Shawl Dance

What's good for the goose, is good for the gander, and the women get their revenge with the Shawl Dance. She must place a shawl somewhere on the body of the man of her choice, and the race is on! No man is exempt from the Shawl Dance. Elders, officials, the announcer, and drummers are all fair game, and are chased with great determination. Once caught, the men must assemble in the arena and perform one of the women's dances. The rest is up to the announcer, and even though he is a man, he shows no mercy on his brothers. If the announcer has been caught, it's his turn to sweat, while a woman takes over as announcer.

By the way, the one who had laughed the hardest at me when I was caught with the hat, got caught himself, with a shawl, at the same pow wow—my husband. Yes, revenge is sweet!

Crow Hop Dance

This dance is often called by the announcer as a penalty for some real or made-up misbehavior. For example, if the announcer feels that some of the men or women did not give it their best effort in the Hat Dance and the Shawl Dance, he can sentence them to a Crow Hop. In this dance, the dancer's body, legs, and feet mimic the motions of a crow hopping around on the ground. Its difficult. If you think there's nothing to it, give it a try.

Ladies' Choice Dance

This is a calm dance, usually a Two-Step or Social Dance, that gives the women a chance to dance with a man they admire, or someone they haven't seen for a long time, or just to be social and talk quietly for a while. It's a nice, relaxing break in all the action. All these dances are great fun and are done in good humor and a happy spirit.

YOU CAN JOIN IN TOO

Dances for everyone are often called to give the formal dancers a break and to encourage spectators to come into the arena to meet new friends and to feel the heart of the drum. Since it is doubtful that you will be dressed in regalia, women should wear a shawl, or scarf, or even a sweater across their shoulders as a sign of respect for the traditions of the arena and the drum. You should relax, let your feet do their own thing, and enjoy the fellowship. Children are welcome to dance as well. When the announcer calls everyone to the arena to join in, go; don't be self-conscious or shy; you're among friends.

Inter-Tribal Dance

Everyone joins in on this one. The dance is done in a line which winds around the arena. Your footwork is not important, and you will soon find a step that is comfortable for you. There is no right or wrong step to this, and if you should get turned around, and start in the wrong direction, someone will change your direction.

Round Dance

This dance is done shoulder to shoulder with everyone facing the center of the arena. Everyone is welcome. You step with your left foot and slide your right foot. Your left leg does all the work and will soon feel like it's about to fall off! You'll soon see just how out of shape you really are.

Friendship Dance

Again, there is no right or wrong footwork, and everyone is encouraged to take part. There are two circles; one moving clockwise, the other counter-clockwise. As the circles pass each other, everyone shakes hands with the person they are facing. This is the perfect time to say a few words of encouragement to a dancer you admire, or to tell someone how beautiful their regalia is. Be real—be human—be kind.

Social Dance or Two Step

This is a couples dance similar to a Grand March. If you decide to join in, or you're invited into the arena by a participant in the pow wow, dance behind a couple who knows what they're doing. The step patterns in this dance depend upon the movements of the couple who are leading the procession, so follow them.

Honoring Dance

From time to time, you will hear the announcer giving information about a family or an individual, and he will call an Honor Dance. These dances are included in the program to recognize an outstanding achievement, such as community work, a new dancer's "coming out," a wedding, a birth, an illness, a death, or any other occasion worthy of special attention.

The Honor Dance is led by the Arena Director and the person being honored. Behind them are the honoree's family members and close friends, followed by all who care to join, including spectators.

The dance begins at the announcer's booth and slowly winds around the arena. As it passes near, those who want to join the procession walk into the arena. They shake the hand of the person being honored and drop a small gift or money into a container being carried by the arena director. They then move to the end of the line and join the dance as it continues its way around the arena.

The Giveaway

The Giveaway is a Native custom as old as time itself and one which should be practiced more by all of us. You may see a Giveaway at a pow wow when someone has an especially joyous occasion to celebrate. A Giveaway is a gift from the heart, from one person to another, and is given to show respect and admiration. The monetary value of this gift is not important. It can be a special stone, a special feather, or anything the giver feels like giving. Nothing is expected by the giver in return.

Sometimes pieces of fruit, treats, small and inexpensive gifts, and other appropriate items are tossed from the arena into the crowd as a way of sharing the happiness. If you see something coming at you, catch it! Another method of Pow Wow Giveaway is for the gifts to be spread on blankets in the center of the arena. Everyone is invited to take an item. You should take this seriously; it is an insult for the gifts not to be taken.

THE AMERICAN INDIAN DANCE THEATRE

While not a pow wow group, The American Indian Dance Theatre is certainly worthy of special attention, because it has brought the spirit and culture of Native American heritage to millions of people around the world. This group was originally formed in the early 1970s as the Native American Theatre Ensemble. It provides the only formal training available to Native Americans interested in dance, theatre, costuming, make-up, lighting, choreography, and even ballet, both classical and modern

The foundation of the troupe's performance comes from traditional ceremonial and pow wow dances which have been stylized into an art form that creates a unique and inspiring theatre experience. In addition, short stories, myths, and legends have been choreographed and set to music. The ancient tales they depict are told with beauty and grace.

The American Indian Dance Theatre presents an exciting and educational show that pays tribute to the history of the indigenous people of our country. If they are appearing near you, I strongly recommend that you go; you'll thank me for the tip.

IV
Feathers

Pawnee Man

FEATHERS

Feathers are important to Native Americans, particularly from birds honored by their tribe, and birds that carry a message for an individual. You will see feathers everywhere at a pow wow, and on everything, especially the regalia of the dancers. Feathers are used in ceremonies and are favored items for a giveaway. They are beautifully wrapped and decorated with beading, fringe, and other things that are special to the person doing the wrapping.

From the earliest of times, feathers have been given as a symbol of honor and respect. Young people were often given an eagle feather when they completed their first vision quest. When you see old photographs of Native Americans holding the long lances with many feathers hanging down from them (coup sticks), and wearing feathers in their hair, or wearing the awesome full feather headdresses, keep in mind that each one of those feathers was earned by its owner. Each feather represents an outstanding deed of kindness, or contribution to the good of the village or the tribe, or outstanding bravery (such as fighting a wild animal), or distinguishing oneself in the hunt, or in battle.

Horses were also honored with feathers. The Nations took great care of their horses, for they knew that their lives depended upon the speed and dependability of the horse. It gave them freedom of movement and allowed them to track their enemies and find their food. They painted their horses with sign language and outfitted them with fancy blankets and beadwork. A horse could earned its own feathers which were carefully tied into the mane and tail.

Many of the feather headdresses and other feather decorations you see on regalia have been handed down through the generations, and have a value that cannot be measured. Here are some of the most commonly seen feathers, and the meanings they have to many Native Nations.

The Eagle

Eagle feathers are the most prized feather of all. The eagle is man's messenger who flies closest to the Great Spirit and who carries man's thoughts and prayers. The eagle is a warrior bird who will fight for food and protect its young. He represents clear vision and keeping the mind and eyes open for the big picture without becoming opinionated or developing tunnel vision.

The bald eagle is a fishing bird who is found near the oceans, lakes, and large streams where fish are plentiful. The tail feathers of the adult bald eagle are white.

The most sought after eagle feather is from the golden eagle sometimes called the spotted eagle because the young birds have white tail feathers with markings of dark brown, or dark grey, or black. Once the bird matures, its tail feathers match the rest of its body, a warm, golden brown. It is a hunting bird found where there is a plentiful supply of snakes, gophers, rabbits, and other small game.

The Owl

The poor owl has gotten a bad rap, for some people look upon it as a bad luck omen. Truth is, the great majority of Native Nations honor the owl, and only a very few tribes consider it a signal of impending death. Those that fear it believe that when an owl is seen or head, someone is about to die. They say the owl comes to carry the soul of the recently deceased safely to the Great Spirit.

Owls range in size from the very small ones that live inside desert cactus, to the large and mighty Great Horned Owl. They are considered by some tribes to be a symbol of wisdom and the ablility to see into a situation to find the truth; they are a sign of strong intuition and the courage to follow that intuition, and are seen as being alert and aware of all that is around them.

The Hawk

The hawk is the messenger, the carrier of signs and messages from the Great Spirit. Hawk reminds us to pay close attention to the details of what is around us and to be aware of the consequences of what we do. They also are a messenger in our thoughts, words, and actions. The shrill scream of the hawk is a reminder to be alert and to experience the wonder of the people and things in our lives.

Hawks live among us and have the ablity to survive in cities, suburban areas, as well as the country. Are they telling us to look at what we're doing to the earth and to ourselves? A tail feather of the great Red Tailed Hawk is a prized possession and is truly beautiful.

The Crow

In some Native beliefs the Crow is a powerful creature, for it is the keeper of the Sacred Laws of the Universe. It has the power to blend darkness and light, and sees the past, present, and future, along with both inner and outer reality. It is the sign of change.

The Crow is also a great trader. They love bright, shiny objects, and if one takes something, it will often leave something in exchange. Of course, you might not like what it leaves, but it has traded with you!

The Magpie

The magpie is the cousin of the crow and is found mostly in the northwest United States. Many Native Americans consider this bird to be the most intelligent member of the crow family because of its ability to adapt and its social order. Magpies will make use of anything. They teach that we should make good use of what is on hand and make full use of our intelligence. Magpies are a sign of opportunity for advancement and spiritual exploration.

The Pheasant

All the feathers of the pheasant are used, perhaps more than any other bird. Because they are so beautiful, and of such varied sizes, you will find them decorating many Native American items, from pouches to shields. The long and graceful tail feathers are used in headdresses and bustles, especially the headdresses of the Aztec and Mayan dancers.

A symbol of family and fertility, the pheasant originated near the Phasis River in Greece. It is a member of the grouse family, as is our chicken.

Reference

If you would like to learn more about "medicine birds" and their messages, I can heartily recommend *Animal Speak*, by Ted Andrews. It was published in 1994 by Llewellyn Publications, St. Paul, Minnesota. It is an excellent book and one that is readily available.

V
Gifts and Craft Souvenirs

Omaha Man

TRADERS AND VENDORS

Since the beginning of time, people have traded with each other, exchanging everything from food to fur. Native Americans were, and still are, master traders, trading between tribes as well as between Nations.

Native peoples honored each other's talents and did not copy the crafts and art work from other regions. Instead, things made by other tribes and other cultures became prized items for trade. It was quite common to find a Zuni bowl in Minnesota, an Appaloosa horse in Mississippi, or Chumash shell work in Wyoming.

This tradition is still alive today, and every pow wow has traders who have bought Native American items from various parts of the country. You can find Eskimo scrimshaw, Kachina dolls, hides, fur pelts, beads, Navajo rugs, and all sorts of treasures. You can buy a finished product or, if you're talented with your fingers and long on patience, the materials to make your own treasures.

There are also traders who sell something called "Dead Pawn." You'll see pegboards and glass counters loaded with magnificent jewelry, silver and turquoise or coral, and finely worked leather goods, all handmade. When I first encountered these traders, it bothered me that families were forced to give up their prized possessions. Then I learned the interesting history of pawning and its place in the Native culture.

When the Southwest was first being settled, the early non-Native businesses were the traders. The large traders had "lending corners" where money could be borrowed against the more elaborate craft items left for security. This was the first step toward banking institutions, long before there were actual banks established in these areas. These traders provided the only source of quick money for Native Americans. When they could afford to buy back their possessions, they did. Many times, however, the owner decided he didn't want it back, or had made something he liked better, or had passed away, or many other reasons. This led to quite an accumulation of what is known as "dead pawn," which is sold at large pow wows.

There are vendors who sell art, music, books, clothing, and all manner of handcrafted items. Many vendors make their own crafts, and you can watch them at work in their booths. If you're attracted to something, ask what it is and its purpose. You don't want to buy a fertility fetish for your 75 year old Aunt May!

Many vendors and traders make their living on the pow wow trail, and it is an expensive proposition. Not only must they buy the materials to make their crafts, they must pay booth fees, travel costs, and living expenses on the road. They must sell their creations, and you will find fair and competitive pricing. As a general rule prices are better, and value far greater, than you can find in retail outlets which sell Native American goods.

Don't be concerned about the authenticity of the items displayed for sale. Pow wow committees know the vendors, most of whom travel the pow wow trail or do the same event year after year. The committees and promoters are very strict about the quality, variety, and authenticity of the goods sold. Most vendors don't accept credit cards or checks; its "cash and carry" that works.

If you have children with you, PLEASE keep them under control, or leave them with a member of your party who is not shopping. An unruly or careless child can cause a lot of damage, very quickly, to a vendors merchandise. You should also be careful with large, bulky bags and backpacks, which can knock things off the tables and displays as you move around. The booth spaces are small, usually no bigger than ten foot by ten foot. This is a tight squeeze for all that is being shown for sale.

FAVORITE POW WOW SOUVENIRS

There are many beautiful articles that you can purchase to remind you of your pow wow visit. Unless an item is clearly and obviously a childs toy, please remember that you are purchasing a symbol of someone's history and heritage. Much time and care has gone into the making of the crafts offered, and they deserved to be cared for and treated with respect.

Don't be surprised to find booths with crystals and other stones for sale. Many Native Nations use crystals and stones in their ceremonies. If there is not a card or slip of paper explaining how these objects are used, and their meaning, be sure to ask. You'll be surprised.

There is considerable confusion about the difference between a dreamcatcher and a shield, a medicine bag and a pouch, and a lack of understanding about various other objects and their uses. We will discuss here some of the more popular pow wow souvenirs, their meanings, and their proper uses.

Drums

There are many sizes and styles of drums. The cost depends upon the size and the skin it is made from and whether it is decorated and/or painted. There are even kits available with all the materials you will need to make your own.

The most common skin used is deer, but elk, cow, and buffalo hide is also used. The tone of the drum is determined by the type of skin used and by how it is laced or attached to the framework and by the tension. If you are purchasing a drum, it should come with a beater; no, not a drumstick, a beater. You should ask if you can play a rhythm on the drum before making a purchase to make sure the drum has the tone, sound, and resonance that appeals to you.

The skin of a drum will get hard and brittle if it is not properly cared for, so be sure to ask the maker how to care for it properly. If you plan to play it, it will need care. If you plan to hang it on a wall, or place it somewhere else for decoration, don't expect it to sound the same as if it were cared for on a regular basis.

DO NOT EVER LEAVE A DRUM IN A CLOSED UP CAR IN THE SUN. It could be ruined because of the heat. The skin drums react to the weather and temperature, and this effects their sound and resonance. Be sure you tell the vendor the type of climate you live in because this may change the type of care needed. Excessive humidity or moisture will make a drum lose its tension. I held a drumming circle by the ocean once and when I struck my drum all I got was a very dull BURP.

Feathers and Animal Parts

Fish and game regulations change from state to state and sometimes even from county to county. The traders and vendors are aware of these local regulations, so you won't find anything at a pow wow that is not legal to sell. Some states will not allow deer toes, antlers, or anything from deer; some will not allow bear fur, teeth, or claws; some will not allow the shells from certain turtles, and on and on. If you see an item offered for sale, you can be sure it's legal. If you are looking for something specific, and can't find it, ask if it is not permitted there, or if the vendor is simply out of stock.

It is illegal to buy and sell bird of prey feathers almost everywhere. The eagle and hawk feathers you see for sale are painted to simulate bird of prey, they are not authentic—they are created. If you touch the feather you will be able to feel the paint. Some artists are exceptionally good at simulating these feathers, and you would never know they weren't real if you didn't stroke them.

Cradleboards

In the old days, very small children were carried in cradleboards secured snugly out of harm's way. The cradleboards varied in design and materials depending upon the lifestyle of the Nation or tribe and the part of the country they lived in.

In the Great Plains, these cradleboards were made of strong

wood fashioned into two sharply pointed ends that extended over the baby's head. These pointed "stakes" served as "brakes." While on the trail, if the baby bounced off the horse or travois, the sharp ends would catch on a rock, or a bush, or something stationary that would stop it from getting too far away.

In villages, where the people did not travel from place to place, they were made of lighter materials, often bent willow, and had rounded tops. They were designed so the child could be placed on a tree limb or rock and be safely out of the way, and still see everything that was going on.

In some Native cultures a cradleboard stayed with the child through adulthood and was used generation after generation. If a tragedy should occur and the child die, his cradleboard was destroyed and sometimes buried with him.

There are full-sized cradleboards available today, as well as smaller sizes and miniatures. Some even come with small Native dolls in them.

Chokers

Chokers are beautiful neckpieces which fit snugly around the throat. They are made from bone (called hairpipe) or dentalium shells, and can be many rows wide. They are decorated with leather, beads, small stones, shells, feathers, whatever materials were used by the craftsman's tribe.

In the old days, the bone choker was worn only by people who held positions of respect and authority, and when you saw someone wearing a bone choker you knew they spoke the truth. It is said that if anyone wearing a choker spoke an untruth, the choker got tighter and tighter around their throat—thus the name "choker."

It is likely that chokers also had a practical use, for their very design would serve to protect the neck and throat from knives and other sharp objects in battle and from the teeth and claws of animals if attacked.

Breastplates

Breastplates were body armor and were worn for protecting the chest and torso against all types of weapons. The most commonly seen ones have rows and rows of bone joined by leather strips and beads or tiny stones. They are tied around the neck and around the waist to hold them in place, and they are heavy. This is an item you would put in a display case or on the wall, for the only place it would be appropriate to wear would be to a Native American gathering.

Another type is the style favored by the Crow and the Nez Perce, as well as some other Nations. It has rows and rows of small beads which could be made from shells or bone. These beads fall in a graduated mass of individual strands which start small at the neck and which get progressively longer and larger as they move over the chest and torso. Its similar to the popular graduated strings of pearls and other jewelry but with many more beads.

The Medicine Bag

The medicine bag is a small, to medium-small, leather pouch worn around the neck on a thin leather strap. It holds items that are of personal importance to the wearer and keeps the spirit of these items close to the heart. It also provides protection for the person. You must never, NEVER touch a medicine bag that someone is wearing without asking first.

Special horses who had earned the great respect of their owners were often given their own medicine bags to wear around their necks. In many Plains Cultures, when a child was born, its umbilical cord was placed inside a small turtle shell and hung from the cradleboard. When the child was old enough to wear a medicine bag, the turtle shell was placed inside the bag. The umbilical cord was a symbol of the ever present connection to the mother and the respect and honor given to the mother.

Pouches

Pouches are larger leather bags and come in varying sizes;

some are big enough to be worn over the shoulder, and some are big enough to use like a saddle bag on a motorcycle. They are very sturdy and durable and are great for athletes, joggers, and bicycle riders, for the straps of the pouch can be hung from handlebars or strung on a belt or any other place that leaves the hands free. They are big enough to carry keys, drivers license, money, and whatever else you need, without being bulky and in the way.

Mandalas

Mandalas range from ones small enough to hang from a rear view mirror, to the very large ones that will take up a lot of of wall space. They are circular with very ornate decorations of fur, feathers, and beads. They come in many different colors and are very beautiful. Mandalas are kept to bring good luck and prosperity.

Dream Catchers

The most popular single item found at pow wows, outside of the beautiful jewelry, is the dream catcher. They come in every size from small ear rings and necklaces to very large wall hangings. Dream catchers are round and have a strung center that looks like a spider web with feathers hanging from the bottom of the hoop. In the center of the web is a hole. Its purpose is to catch happy dreams and let them slide down the feathers to the sleeping person. The unhappy dreams are sent away through the hole.

Vendors

VI
What You Won't See

Cree Man

SACRED DANCES

There were as many ceremonial dances and dances of prayer as there were tribes in the days before European contact on this continent. Some of those ancient dances have survived and continue to be performed today. As a general rule, these dances are sacred and performed in secluded areas just for the people of the tribe. If you are ever invited to attend such a ceremony, consider yourself a special and honored individual; you have earned the trust of the elders of that tribe.

Dances such as the healing ceremonies of the False Face Society of the Iroquois and the Bladder Dance of the Eskimo are not well-known and have remained rituals sacred to those Nations. However, three sacred dances were seen by non-Native eyes and were so misunderstood and misrepresented that the mere mention of these ceremonies struck fear in the hearts of the white man, especially the military. You will never see these ceremonies at a pow wow, but it is important to understand their purpose and significance to Native People.

The Sun Dance

From the beginning of recorded time, devout believers in a Supreme Being have held numerous ceremonies to seek atonement, to ask forgiveness for the sins of mankind, and to seek blessings for health and good fortune. All religions around the world have, or have had, such rituals.

These ceremonies have ranged from human and animal sacrifices, through the offering of special foods, to the wearing of stiff shirts of untanned animal hide with the hair turned toward the body (hair shirts), to the whipping of oneself with leather or rope whips. The Sun Dance is such a ceremony and is a sacred ritual of Native Americans. Its practice began on the Great Plains, but the movement of Native Americans away from their original homeland has introduced the custom to other parts of the country.

The Sun Dance is a ceremony of self-sacrifice in which both men and women participate, even older children are allowed to dance. There are prayers for the deliverance of all the races, of all creatures of the earth, and for the earth itself. Prayer offerings are made which carry prayers for peace and understanding and prosperity for all peoples of the earth. Each dancer may make personal prayer offerings for family and friends who have passed away, or who may be ill or in need, or who seek a special blessing. The Sun Dancer is saying, "I am my brother's keeper, and I pray for him with my mind, my soul, and my body."

The Sun Dance Ceremony usually lasts four days, and is held in a remote and private site selected by the elders. It is one of the most misunderstood of all Native American ceremonies. Every attempt has been made to outlaw and forbid the Sun Dance since it was first discovered by Europeans. It has always continued despite beliefs to the contrary. It continues today with more dancers, in more locations, than ever before.

The Ghost Dance

During the middle 1800s, many Nations across the Americas had Ghost Dances, performed in ceremony for their own tribal purposes. It was not unusual and no great attention was paid to the ceremonies by the authorities. However, the most famous Ghost Dance of all, and perhaps the last ceremony of its type, gave birth to an uproar which ended in tragedy.

The reservation system was already in place, and the lives and the movements of Native Americans was tightly controlled by the military. It was a time of great deprecation, and it seemed that surely the Red Race would cease to exist.

A Paiute holy man, Wovoka, had a vision in which he was given the details of a Ghost Dance to be performed by all the people. The Ghost Dance was a prayer for the return of the buffalo, the game, and the hunting grounds necessary for the survival of the Red Race. It was a prayer for the return of the wisdom of the elders and the ancient ones, a prayer for a life of harmony and freedom and prosperity. It was a prayer that the white man would leave this land and return to his home in Europe.

Word of Wovoka's vision spread quickly, and many tribes took up this dance of prayer. The increased activity and involvement by so many tribes caused the military people to be fearful. They were sure this was a new "war dance" which signaled the beginning of another "Indian uprising." It was never intended as such, but this fear led to actions which have covered the pages of history with blood. Pilgrimages to Wounded Knee continue today.

The Snake Dance

The Hopi believe that all living things in nature, including man, have a specific job to do in order to keep the world in balance. They have many complex rituals to show the spirit world that the people have good hearts and that they are doing their jobs in the proper way. The most intensely dramatic of these rituals is the Snake Dance, which is essentially a prayer for rain to insure a good harvest. It is usually held in August.

When the Snake Dance was discovered by Europeans, the Hopi were accused of devil worship, black magic, sorcery, and all manner of evil practices. Such a furor broke out across the country that the ceremony was closed to outsiders. All photographs have been forbidden since 1914. To this day, this ritual remains closed to outsiders, and the ban on photographs now covers drawings, sketches, and renditions of all types. The illustration of the Snake Dancer in this book is the artist's interpretation of written descriptions and old photographs taken at the turn of the century, before the ban was imposed.

The Snake Dance ceremony lasts for nine days and is performed by members of the Antelope Society and the Snake Society, which are Hopi religious groups. During the first several days, the members engage in prayer and the making of prayer sticks. They also gather snakes from the surrounding desert. Once collected, these snakes, both poisonous and non-poisonous, are taken into the kiva (an underground ceremonial room) where the men are preparing for the final ritual. They are kept there for the nine days in a bower built of small trees and bushes.

On the eighth day the members of the Antelope Society begin the dancing by circling the village plaza holding food from the early harvest, such as beans, melons, squash, etc. Early on the ninth day, the snakes in the kiva are washed in water and dried with sand. It is believed that the snakes can tell if a man has a truly pure and fearless heart. After their bath and cleansing, they drape themselves over the most worthy man to sleep.

At sunset on the ninth day, the final ceremony begins with the appearance of the Antelope and Snake Dancers. They are dressed in regalia that has not changed for centuries, with bodies painted in the colors of rain clouds, lightening, and rain. The Antelope Dancers chant while the Snake Dancers retrieve the snakes, one at a time, from the bower where they have been resting. A snake is placed in the mouth of each dancer who then dances one complete circle around the village plaza.

Each Snake Dancer is accompanied by a "hugger" whose job it is to keep the snake from striking and biting. It is believed that snakes are terrified of eagles, so each hugger carries a snake "whip" made of several eagle feathers. He strokes the snake with this feather whip to keep it calm and docile.

Once the circle around the plaza has been completed, the snake is placed on the ground, and a third man gathers it up and hands it to an Antelope Dancer to hold until the ceremony is over. Each snake in the bower is danced with in this fashion until the bower is empty. When the last circle has been completed, the chief Snake Dancer draws a circle of sacred cornmeal on the earth, and all snakes are placed into this circle. A final dance is performed around the cornmeal circle, and the nine-day ceremony is closed with the return of the snakes to the desert.

It is believed that the snakes carry the prayers of the Hopi for rain and an abundant harvest and that they intercede with the spirit world to grant these prayers. Many years of reports tell of thunderstorms and cloudbursts following the conclusion of the Snake Dance ceremony.

Sun Dancer

Snake Dancer

VII
In Closing

Horse Race

Finding A Pow Wow

Most colleges and universities have a Native American Studies Department or a Native American Club on campus. These are excellent sources for pow wow information, for they usually receive flyers about pow wows in their area. There are national and regional pow wow calendars which are published independently. Native American newspapers and magazines usually publish pow wow schedules. Those of you who have discovered Cyberspace, and are on the Internet, could subscribe to the Native-L mailing list and check out the Alt.Native Newsgroup. These are great sources of information on pow wows, and if you don't see anything near you, post the question. Someone on the network will be happy to give you information. The Web pages for Native Net, Powersource, and The People's Page, among many other Native pages you will discover, are very informative.

Sometimes pow wows are advertised in main stream newspapers, but not often. However, the public relations person at any large newspaper should have information on pow wows in their area.

If you want to catch a pow wow while on vacation, call the Travel and Tourism Bureau in the State Capitol of each state you'll be passing through, and check the Internet sources mentioned above. Almost every state, without exception, has at least one major pow wow during the year.

A complete listing of pow wows and gatherings in the U.S. and Canada could, and does, fill a book. I highly recommend the annual *Pow Wow Calendar* as the most complete guidebook to Native American events available. You can order a copy by calling The Book Publishing Company at 1-800-695-2241.

Once you find your first pow wow, you're home free. Flyers announcing other pow wows are always available at the announcer's booth and in many vendor booths.

HOWEVER, no matter where you get pow wow scheduling information, be sure to verify the dates and locations before making the trip. Many things can happen to cause a pow wow to change its location and/or dates, so be wise and make sure the information is still accurate.

SEE YOU ON THE POW WOW TRAIL.

War Pony

About the Author

Julia White is my Anglo name, and my ancient Sioux name is Meyna Hahn-a'ae. I am a mixed-breed Native American, being 1/4 German, 1/4 Sioux, and 1/2 Cherokee. My birthplace is North Carolina, as was my family's, making me an Eastern Band Cherokee and a descendant of the Ancient Sioux who originated in North Carolina.

My Native heritage was unknown to me until about ten years ago. On my journey down the "Red Road" I stumbled upon pow wows and their magic. The information in this book comes from my years on the pow wow trail, from conversations with my Native friends and from endless pestering of elders and pow wow officials.

Connecting Link Magazine carries my column on the Native American, and I am a staff writer for *If It Doesn't Grow Corn*, a Native newspaper based in Sacramento, California. Additionally, I teach classes and seminars called "Meet The Native American" and "Native American Awareness." These gatherings are held to share little known information about the history and lives of the First Peoples of the Americas, in an effort to build awareness and understanding. These gatherings are not, and will never be, platforms for political views or social commentary. They are journeys into a time and a life-style which are no more.

Those of you who travel the Internet can find my on-going articles about Native women of history, a series called "Woman Spirit" at a Web Site called "Power Source Gallery," and in their magazine, *Talking Leaf*. The Web site address for Power Source Gallery is: http://www.powersource.com/powersource/ Also a series on animal energies and articles of interest to the general public can be found at the Oracle Web site http://www.idirect.com/oracle/library/library.html

Additionally, my on-going classes, questions and answers, and general discussions are at a Web site, called "The People's

Page," in the education section of that publication. The Web site address for The People's Page is: http://www.cris.com/~nlthomas I would like to hear from you; if you have e-Mail, I can be reached at Meyna@ix.netcom.com

My sincere thanks to Diana Stanley for taking the time from her busy schedule to do the paintings and illustrations for *The Pow Wow Trail*. For additional information on my classes or my books, or on the works of Visionary Artist Diana Stanley, write to either of us at 3285 Park Lane, Long Beach, CA 90807, or call (310) 490-0344.

MAY YOU WALK IN PEACE AND HARMONY.

Julia

About the Artist

Diana Elizabeth Stanley is a native Californian of Lenni-Lenape (Delaware) heritage. She began painting at the age of two and has supported herself through her art most of her life.

Diana's fine art has been collected around the world for many years. It is on exhibit and available, in both limited edition and open edition prints, from Four Winds Publishing, Whittier, CA; (310) 695-5259, The Fusion Gallery and Art Center in Richmond, VA, and A Class Act (Two) Gallery in La Conner, WA. She also has greeting cards available from Spirit Art Cards, Edina, MN; (800) 523-5831, and two series of collector plates from The Bradford Exchange, Niles, IL; (708) 966-2770.

Her work can be seen on many book covers and magazine illustrations, puzzles, T-shirts, mugs; on a regular basis in *Connection Link Magazine*; on continuing display at The People's Page on The World Wide Web, in the Native American Art Gallery Section; and on the Web site http://www.newageinfo,com/ In addition, she was commissioned by The Marshall Islands and The Republic of Micronesia to create the art for their 1996 series of stamps.

Favorite Horse

Order Your Own

Pow Wow Calendar 1997

Guide to Pow Wows and Gatherings U.S.A. & Canada

A definitive guide and schedule for Native American pow wows, dances, craft fairs, and cultural events to be held in 1997 around the United States and Canada.

Each entry includes: type of event, date, location, phone number, and contact person. An introduction includes cultural facts and important information for craft vendors.

Order Information

Available mid-November 1996 from:

Book Publishing Co.
P.O. Box 99
Summertown, TN 38483
800-695-2241

Please enclose check or money order for:
$11.95 per book ($8.95 + $2.50 shipping).

Canadian Orders
Enclose a Canadian postal union money order for:
$11.95 - US ($8.95 + $3.00 shipping).

Team Dancers

These fine Native American books are available from your local bookstore or from the publisher.

Book Publishing Co.
PO box 99
Summertown, TN, 38483
1-800-695-2241
$2.50 shipping per book

Cherokee Titles

American Indian Coloring Book $3.50
Arts & Crafts of the Cherokee $9.95
Aunt Mary Tell Me a Story $3.95
Cherokee A-B-C Coloring Book $3.50
Cherokee Past & Present, The $3.95
Cherokee Plants $3.95
Finger Weaving $4.95
How to Make Cherokee Clothing $23.95
Seven Clans of the Cherokee People $3.95
Story of the Cherokee People, The $3.95

Native American Titles

Basic Call to Consciousness $7.95
Blackfoot Craftworkers Book $11.95
Chants & Prayers $9.95
Children of the Circle $9.95
Daughters of Abya Yala $8.95
Dream Feather $11.95
Eyes of Chief Seattle, The $16.95
Good Medicine Collection, A $9.95
Guide to Native American Music Recordings, A $12.95
How Can One Sell the Air? $6.95
Indian Tribes of the Northern Rockies $9.95
Legends Told by the Old People $5.95
Native American Crafts Directory $8.95
Natural Education, A $8.95
Powwow 1996 Calendar $8.95
Pow Wow Trail, The $8.95
Sacred Song of the Hermit Thrush $5.95
Song of the Seven Herbs $11.95
Song of the Wild Violets $5.95
Spirit of the White Bison $5.95
Teachings of Nature $8.95
The People $5.95
Traditional Dress $6.95